AF572502

On an average day, there are many exciting things that Aden and his friends can do. But on this specific occasion, Aden decided to spend time making new adventures and memories with his mom.

"Aden take the Train" will take you on an amazing ride filled with memorable moments that all children and parents can relate too!

Aden Takes the Train

Cristian Randle
Aden Kelley

One day mom and Aden
were trying to
find something to do for the weekend.
Then Mommy thought
"Let's take a train ride!"
They had never ridden a train before and
they were both very excited.

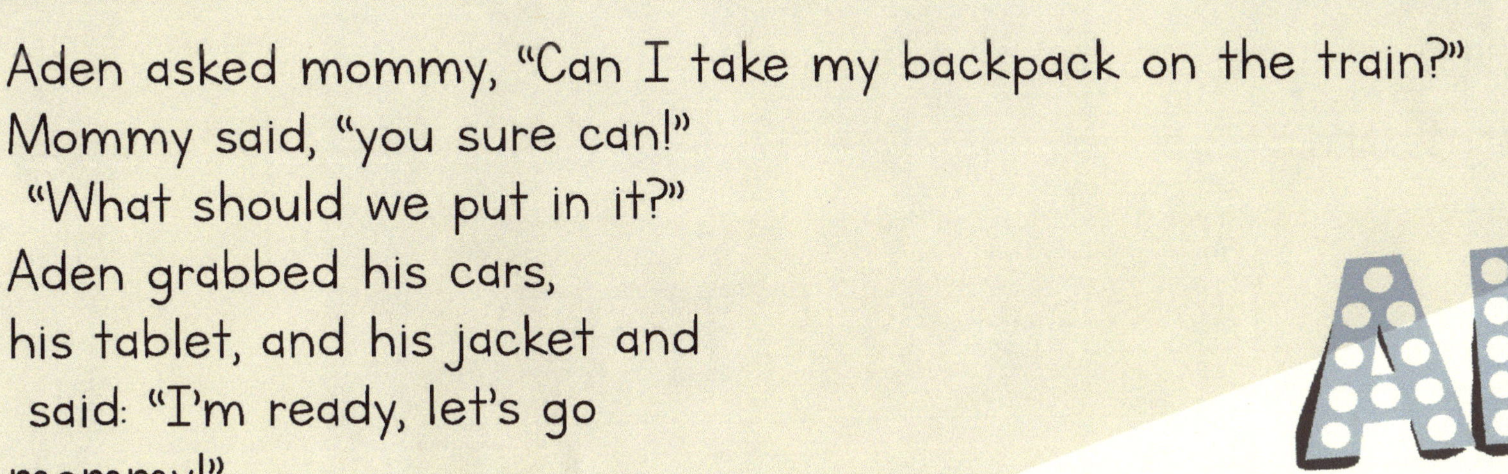

Aden asked mommy, "Can I take my backpack on the train?"
Mommy said, "you sure can!"
"What should we put in it?"
Aden grabbed his cars,
his tablet, and his jacket and
said: "I'm ready, let's go
mommy!"

"Tomorrow", mommy explained,
Aden so was so eager he could not wait!

Early the next morning they, set off on their adventure. Careful not to wake Papa, they gathered their things and were off to the train station.

Once they arrived there was so much to do.
First was finding where to park, then
where to buy the tickets, lastly where to board, and where they will be sitting.
As they entered the station they found the ticket counter.

To greet them was a friendly man who could answer all their questions.

While mommy was
getting things set,
Aden was able to observe all the
interesting things that happen
at the train station.

He saw toy trains behind a window. Kids nestled tightly in their parent's arms resting, and families sitting and waiting for their train to arrive. Aden also saw workers pushing and pulling bags on carts.

Then a man came out and said,

"All Aboard."....

"Mommy who is that?", Aden asked. "Well it's the train conductor", said mommy.

"Hello young man, is this your first time on a train?" "Yes," Aden replied in a soft voice. "How about we make you a conductor for the day?".

Aden looked with confusion, then he seen something come from behind the man's back. The nice man said, "All train conductors must have a special hat!"

Aden said thank you with great excitement. Then, he and mommy boarded the train.

Settled in their seats, the train began to
move and everyone could hear Aden

Shout, "choo, choo".
As they rode, they enjoyed sights.
From trees to rivers and many
bright lights.

Aden played with toys and
pulled out his tablet.
The concierge, came around and
offered them snacks.
He also gave them a tourist pack.

Before they knew it, there was a sudden delay. There was freight train on the tracks blocking the train's way. They waited and waited and waited some more. It seemed like their fun adventure was fun no more.

To make it back home, they had to adjust their trip.

Instead of St. Louis, they stopped in Kirkwood to stretch for a bit.

Here, Aden and mom were able to explore life from a smaller city.

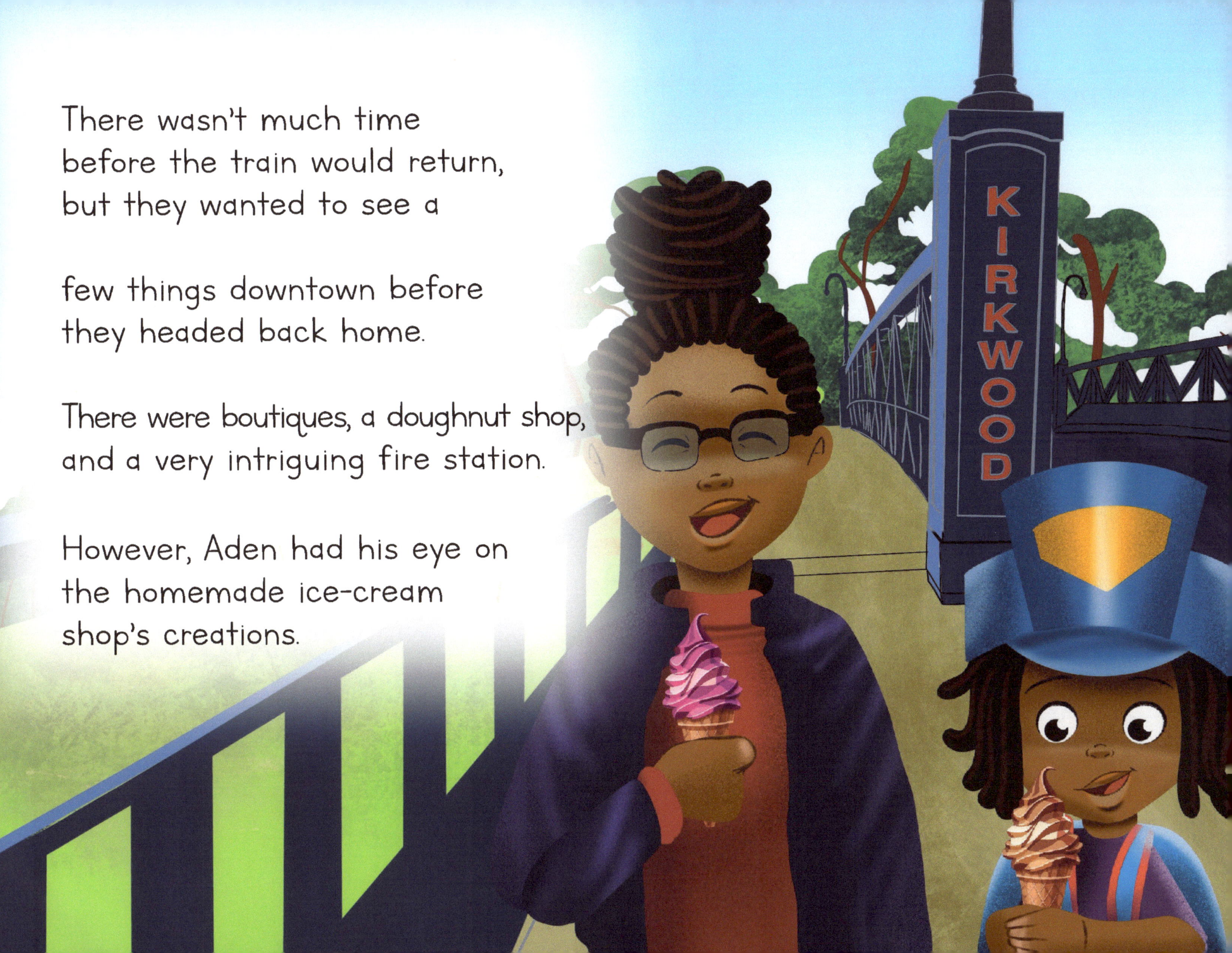

There wasn't much time
before the train would return,
but they wanted to see a

few things downtown before
they headed back home.

There were boutiques, a doughnut shop,
and a very intriguing fire station.

However, Aden had his eye on
the homemade ice-cream
shop's creations.

"May I have some chocolate, Mommy?"
Aden asked,
as they came to the window.

They got ice cream, walked to the park, and
enjoyed the sounds and people of

the small town.

Back at the train station, everyone awaited the train.

"There it is, there it is," Aden shouted as the train pulled in, with lights shining bring for all to see.

Still wearing his conductor hat, Aden spoke to the crowd, "All Aboard!" Behind

him a man stated, "yes, all aboard, tickets please".

With a smile from ear to ear Aden and mommy got back on the train for their adventure was coming to an end.

The ride home was much more quiet and smooth.

A day full of travel caused them to become very tired. As the sun went down, and the train moved through the cities, Aden and mom slept peacefully in their seats dreaming of the fun and new people they met.

The train came to a stop.
They were home at last. Mommy asked,
"how was your
first train ride?".

Aden looked up and said, "it was a blast!".

Aden takes the Train

Aden takes the Train

Special Thanks

Thank you for supporting early reading in children. It is our goal to promote early learning and encourage children to practice early literacy skills while gaining a passion for enjoying a great story in a book.

CPSIA information can be obtained
at www.ICGtesting.com
Printed in the USA
BVHW062354150320
574932BV00001BA/1

* 9 7 8 0 5 7 8 6 5 0 1 9 7 *